Handwriting Practice For Kids

1	2	3	4	5	6
1	2	3	4	5	6
1	2	3	4	5	6
1	2	3	4	5	6
1	2	3	4	5	6
1	2	3	4	5	6
1	2	3	4	5	6
1	2	3	4	5	6

Numbers & Shapes Handwriting Practice
Workbook Sheets

Handwriting Number Practice

Beginners

one

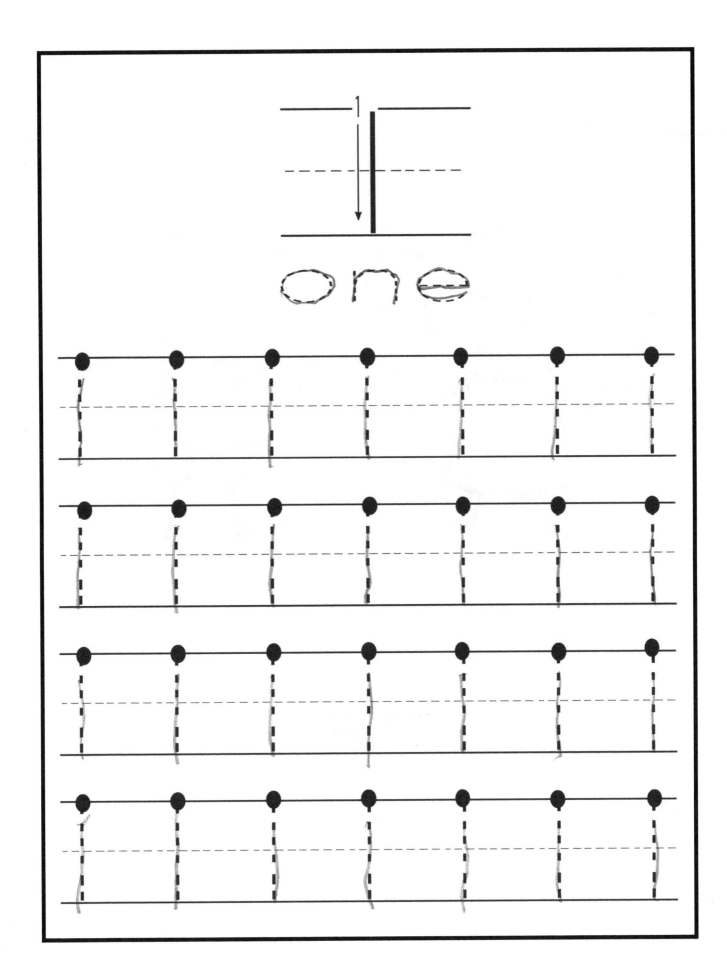

two

2

two

three

$\overset{1}{\underset{2}{3}}$

three

3 3 3 3 3

3 3 3 3 3

3 3 3 3 3

3 3 3 3 3

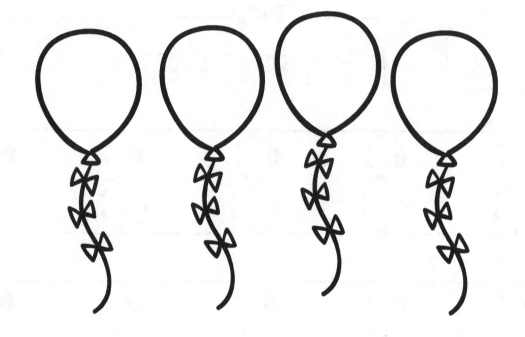

four

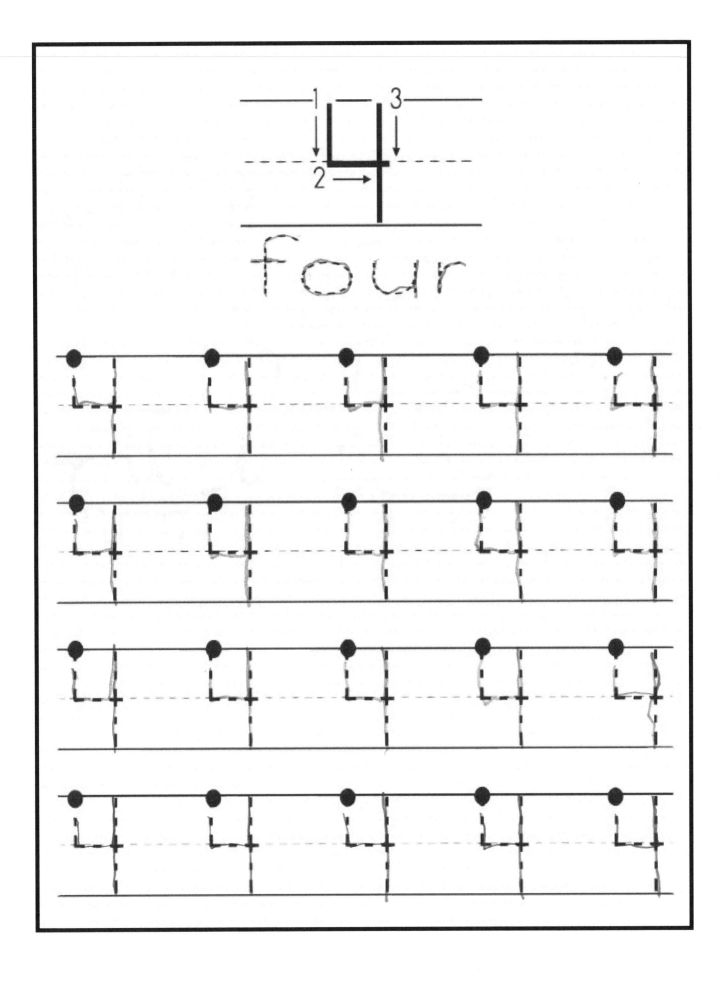

five

5

five

six

6

six

seven

7

seven

eight

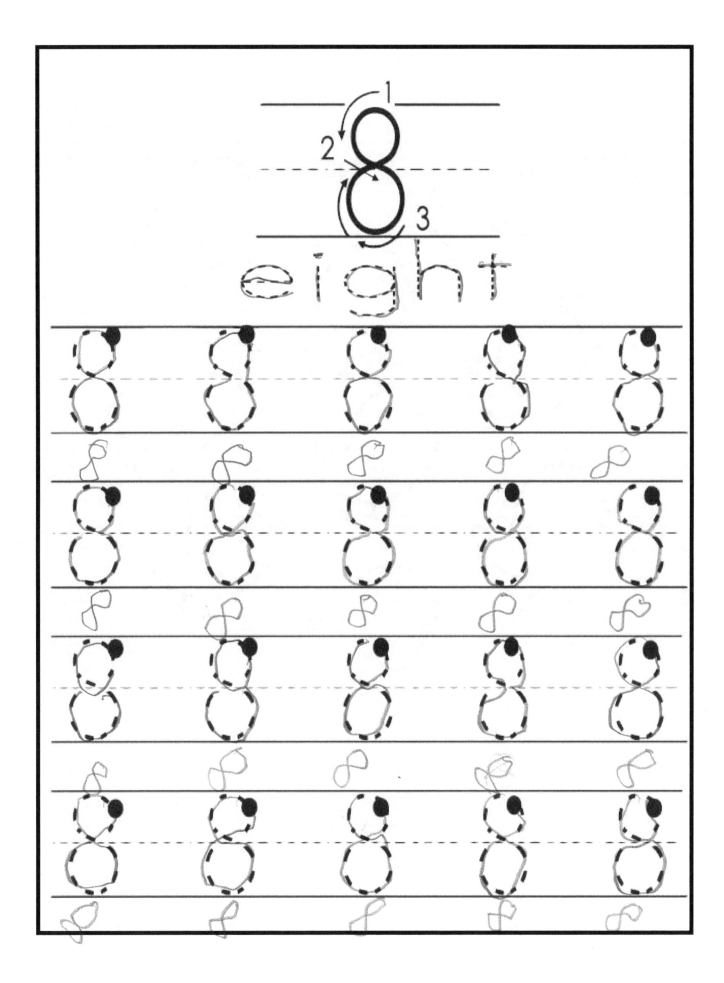

nine

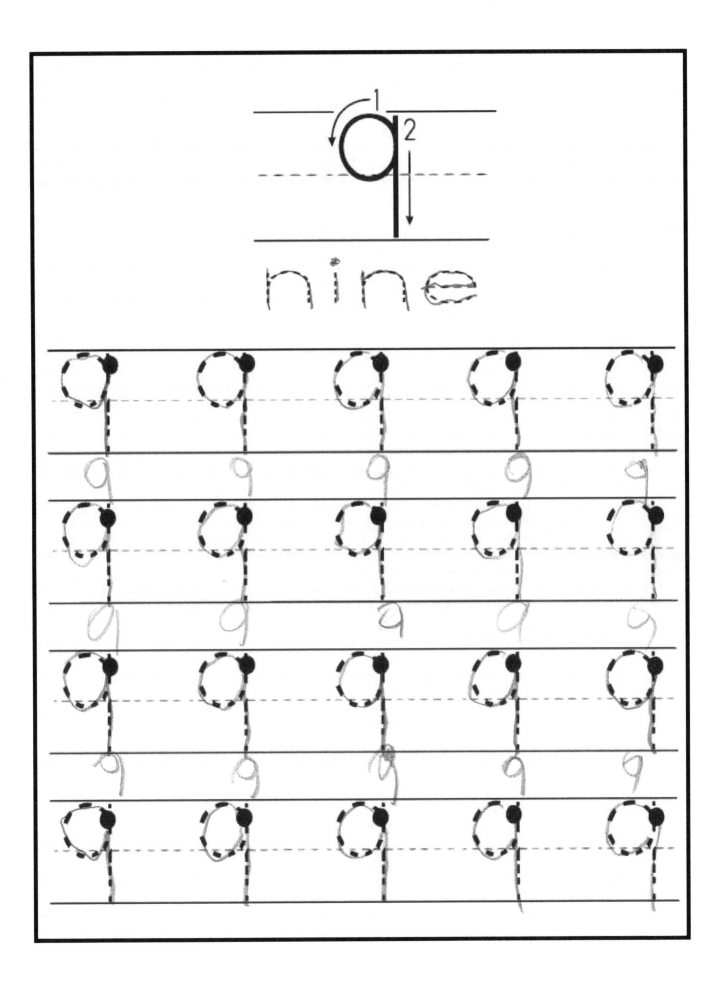

nine

Handwriting Number Practice

Write the letters freehand
and color the pictures

one

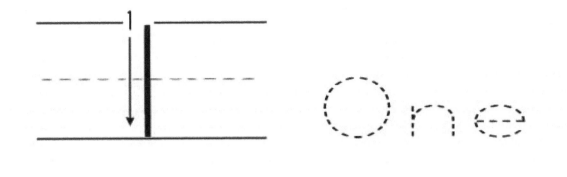

Two

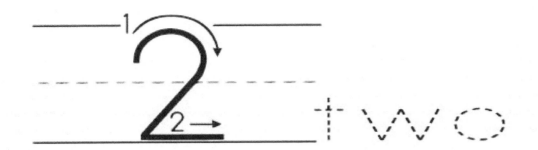

2 two

2

2

2

2

2

2

three

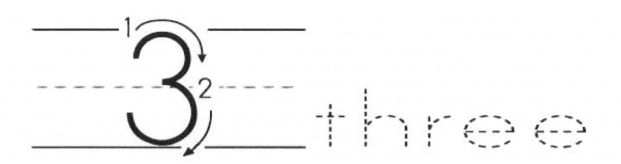

three

3
3
3
3
3
3

four

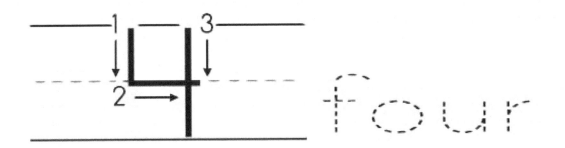

four

five

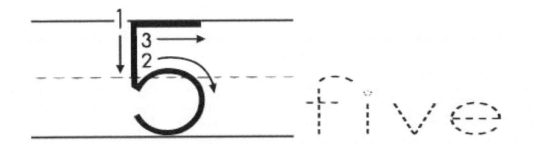

5 five

six

six

seven

7 seven

eight

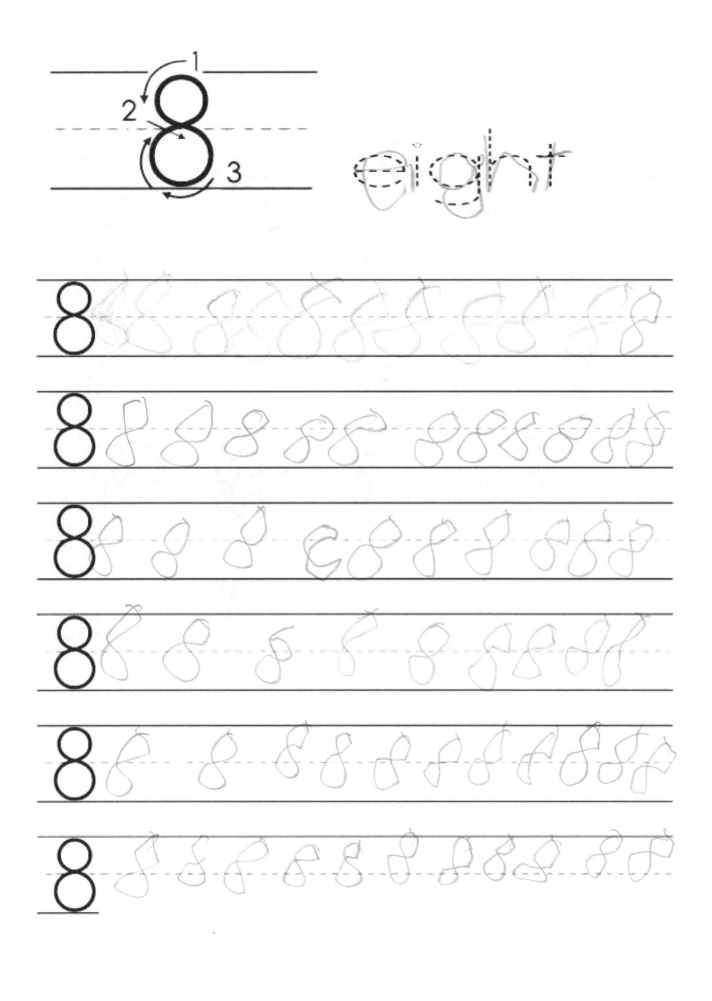

nine

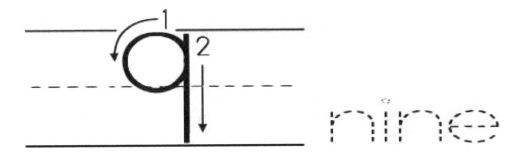

q q q q q q q q q q q

q q q q q q q q q q q q

q q q q q

ZERO

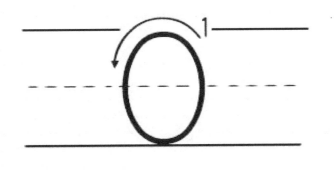

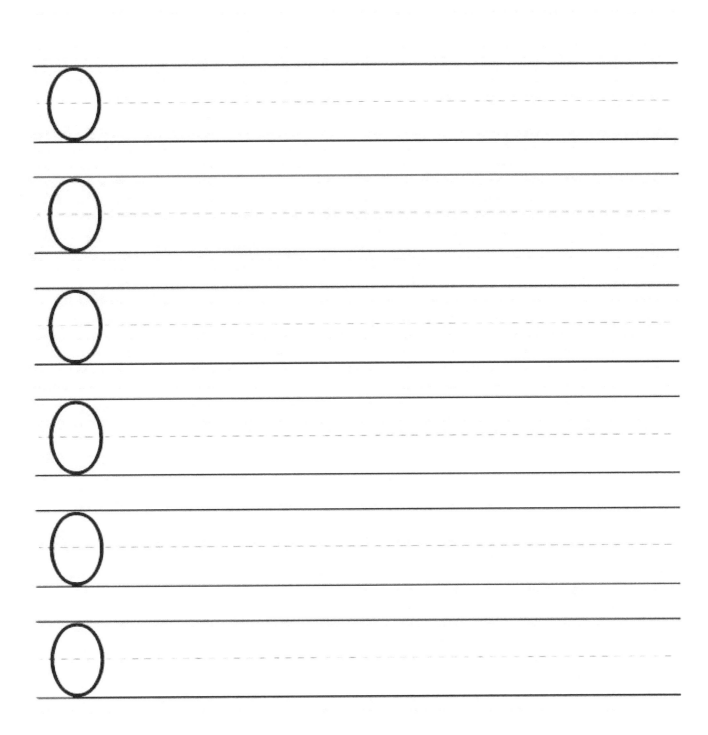

Shapes

Trace around the shapes and their names

circle
circle

square

square

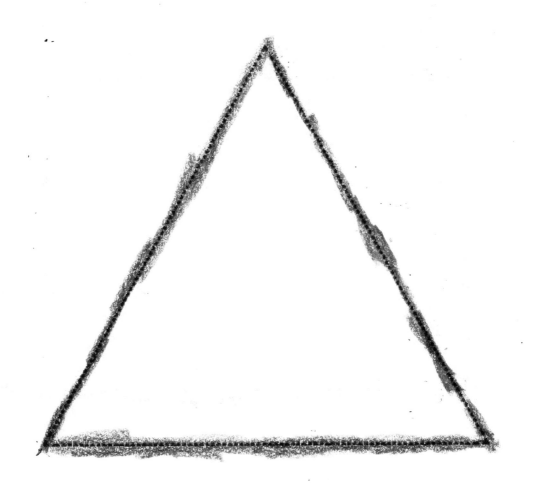

triangle
triangle

rectangle

rec t an gle

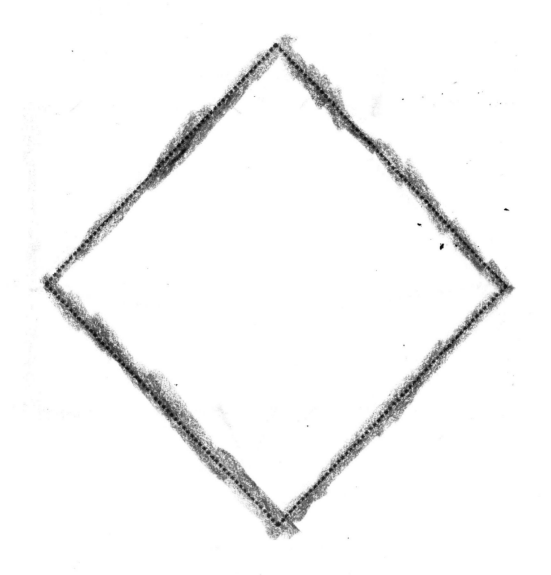

diamond

diamond

star

st ar

(rhombus)

(rhomb us)

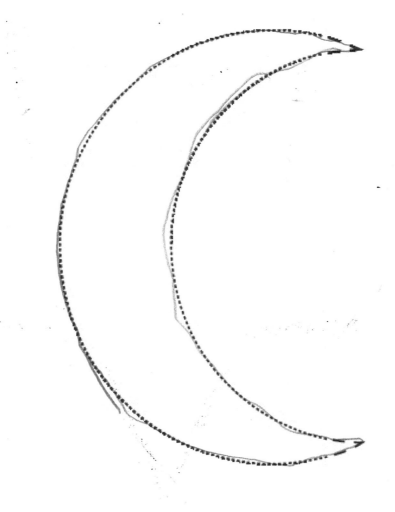

Moon

Moon

(crescent)

(crescent)

heart

heart

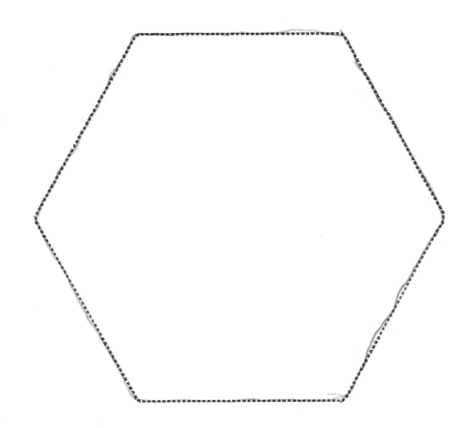

hexagon

hexagon

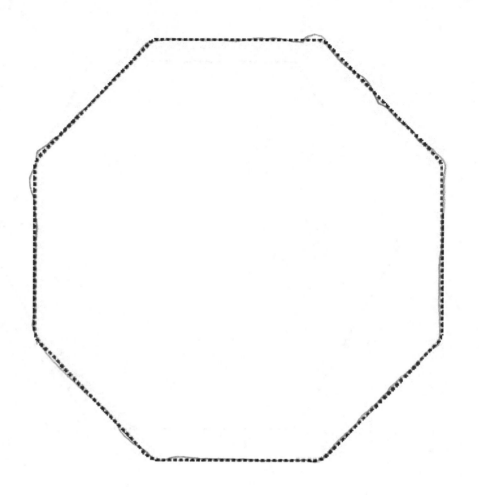

octagon

octagon

Color the
Numbers 1-10

and trace the words

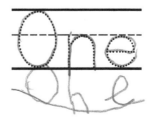

two

two

Three
Three

Four

Foar

Five
Five

Six
Six

Seven
seven

Eight

Eight

Ten

Blake~

Happy Exploring!

Autographed
Copy

Thank you to everyone who helped us save KeeKee's life in 2012!
Stephanie Frederick, *While You're Away*
Dr. Lara Bartl, Dr. Jenifer Farrell & Team,
VCA Alexandria Animal Hospital
Terri Grow & Team, *Pet Sage*
We're forever grateful!

Published by Calithumpian Press, LLC
CalithumpianPress.com

Book designed by Paul Williams and edited by Lisa Pliscou.

The text in this book is Neutraface by House Industries.
The font for the title is called Elroy.

The Nutella® hazelnut spread name and packaging are registered
trademarks of Ferrero U.S.A., Inc. Use of the product name and image
does not imply any affiliation with or endorsement by them. It does imply
an affinity, because we know there just isn't a better way to enjoy a crêpe
but with Nutella hazelnut spread on it!

First Edition – 2013

Library of Congress Control Number: 2013902059
Cataloging-In-Publication Data available

ISBN: 978-0-9886341-0-7

Printed in the United States of America
by Lehigh Phoenix, Hagerstown, Maryland

10 9 8 7 6 5 4 3 2 1... up, up, and away!

www.KeeKeesBigAdventures.com

CALITHUMPIAN
PRESS

KeeKee's Big  Adventures
in Paris, France

Story by Shannon Jones
Illustrations by Casey Uhelski

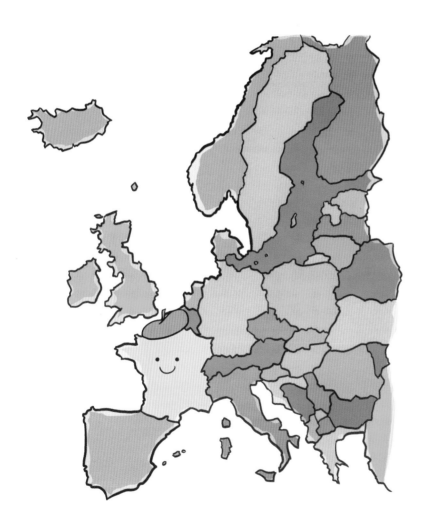

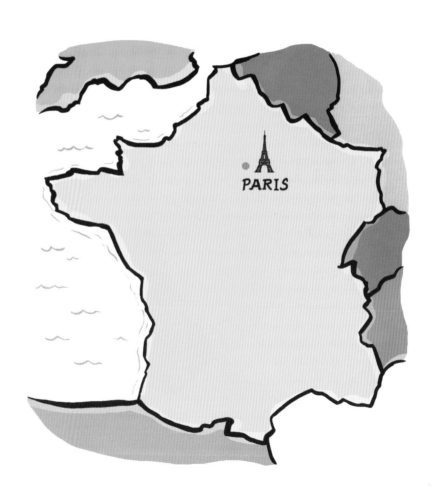

PARIS

"Whoa!" shouted KeeKee.
"What was *that*?"
She peered below the clouds
and spotted something pointy.

"Ooh là là! I made it to Paris! And looks like I can check the first thing off my list..."

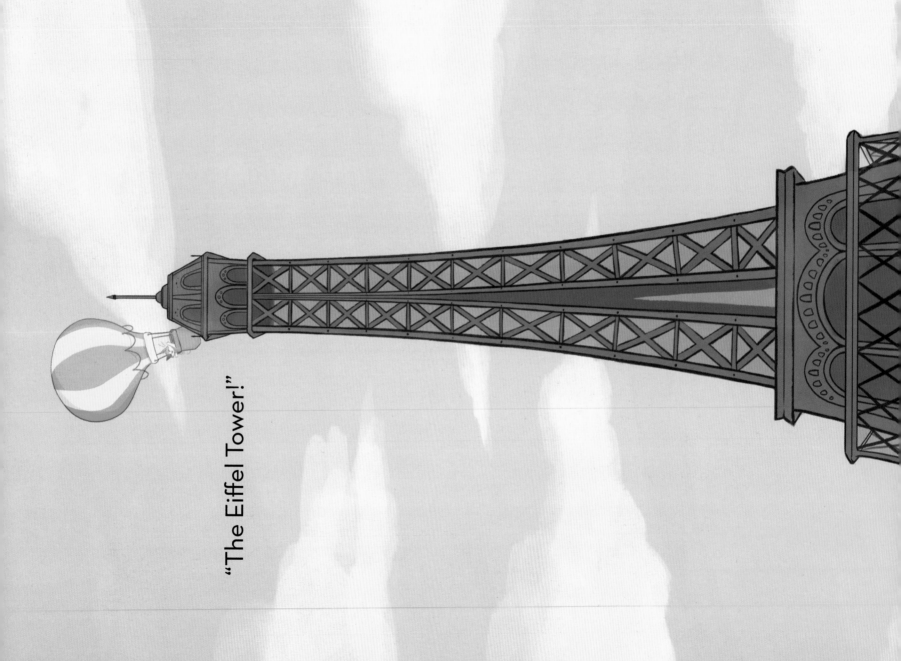

"The Eiffel Tower!"

"*Bonjour, Mademoiselle!*" said Elliot the seagull. "*Bienvenue!* Welcome to the City of Lights."

"*Merci!*" said KeeKee. "It's been my *dream* to visit Paris! I've always wanted to..."

"Climb the Eiffel Tower. *Check!*"

Visit the beautiful Notre Dame Cathedral.

And see the *Meowna Lisa* painting."

Elliot offered to show KeeKee the way, and they strolled down the magnificent Champs-Élysées, one of the most famous streets in the world.

Inside the majestic Tuileries Garden, KeeKee admired the beautiful flowers. Odilia, the duck, introduced herself as the gardener.

"How spectacular!" said KeeKee.

"*Merci beaucoup!*" said Odilia.

Suddenly KeeKee's nose twitched.
"What's that yummy smell?"
she asked eagerly.

"Why, that's my favorite *crêperie!*" Elliot answered. "Would you like to try a real French *crêpe?*"

"Yes, please!" KeeKee exclaimed. There were so many choices!

Elliot ordered his usual salmon *crêpe.*

"I love *jambon et fromage* – ham and cheese, a *croque-monsieur crêpe,*" said Odilia.

"A *crock monster?*" said KeeKee.

She studied the menu, and said, "May I please have a Nutella and banana *crêpe?*"

The *crêpes* were scrumptious!
They gobbled down every last bite.

KeeKee invited Odilia to come
along to Notre Dame.

"I'd love to!" answered Odilia.
"You *must* see the gargoyles!"

KeeKee gazed up at Notre Dame Cathedral in awe. It was huge!

"Do you see the gargoyles?" said Odilia. "Let's get a closer look."

"Who can make the funniest gargoyle face?!" said KeeKee.

They climbed the 387 steps to the top of the towers.

"KeeKee, you definitely win!" Elliot said.

Still giggling,
the friends made their way to the
Louvre Museum.

and paintings...

They looked
at sculptures...

until they finally came to...

"Wait a minute!" KeeKee exclaimed.
"The *Mona Lisa*?"

She made her way through the crowd
to get a closer look.

"Do you have a question, *Mademoiselle*?" asked Bertrand, the security guard dog.

"I thought this painting was called the *Meowna Lisa*," replied KeeKee. "I was expecting a cat!"

"*Non, non, Mademoiselle*," Bertrand said. "This is the world-famous *Mona Lisa* – a lady!"

He smiled at KeeKee. "But if you're looking for the *Meowna Lisa*, I think I can help you."

Bertrand led the way across town, to the highest point in Paris... Montmartre.

The funicular was a fun way to get to the top.

In the famous artists' square,
Bertrand spotted painter pooch Pierre.

"Pierre, *mon ami!*" Bertrand greeted him.
"My friend KeeKee is interested in a *Meowna Lisa*."

"*Oui oui*, KeeKee! Please sit down for me!" Pierre said.

In no time at all, he skillfully painted KeeKee her very own *Meowna Lisa*.

voilà!

"*Merci beaucoup!*" KeeKee said, thrilled. "It's lovely!"

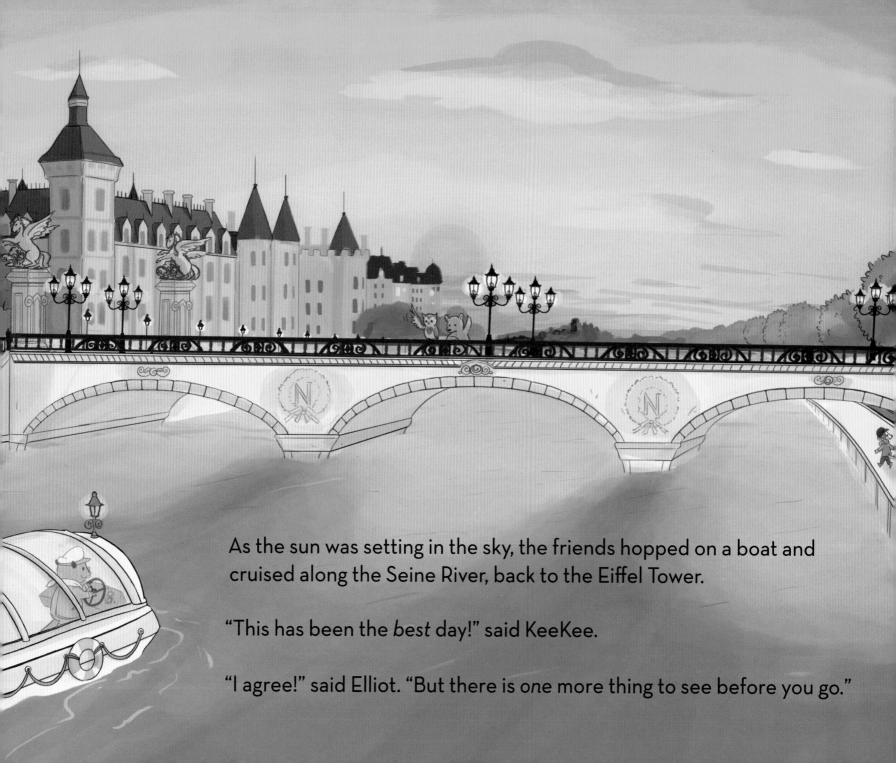

As the sun was setting in the sky, the friends hopped on a boat and cruised along the Seine River, back to the Eiffel Tower.

"This has been the *best* day!" said KeeKee.

"I agree!" said Elliot. "But there is *one* more thing to see before you go."

The Eiffel Tower began
to sparkle with the most
beautiful, twinkly lights.

The friends gazed up
with delight.

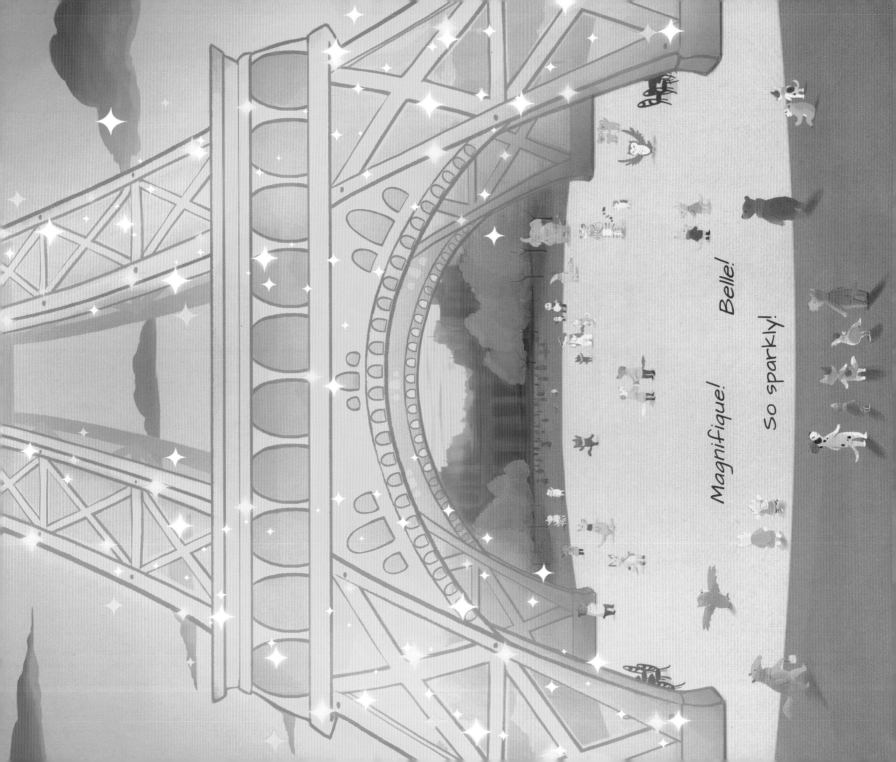

Magnifique!

Belle!

So sparkly!

At last, proudly clutching the *Meowna Lisa* under her arm, KeeKee climbed the tower, hopped into the basket, and untied her balloon.

And she floated...

up into the sky...

Pronunciation Guide & Glossary

Words & Phrases

Au revoir .... (oh ruh-VWAHR) .... Goodbye

Belle .... (behl) .... Beautiful

Bienvenue .... (be-awn-vuh-NEW) .... Welcome

Bon voyage .... (bone vwa-YAHGE) .... Have a good trip

Bonjour .... (bone-ZHOOR) .... Hello / good morning

Croque-monsieur (croak muh-SYUH) .... Grilled ham & cheese

Crêpe .... (krehp) .... Thin pancake

Crêperie .... (krehp-uh-REE) .... Crêpe restaurant

Fromage .... (froh-MAHJ) .... Cheese

Jambon .... (ZHAN-bone) .... Ham

Mademoiselle .... (mad-mwah-ZEL) .... Miss

Magnifique .... (mahg-nee-FEEK) .... Magnificent

Merci .... (mare-SEE) .... Thank you

Merci beaucoup ... (mare-SEE boe-KOO) ... Thank you very much

Miaou .... (mee-yow) .... Meow

Mon ami .... (mohn ah-MEE) .... My friend

Non .... (nohn) .... No

Ooh là là .... (oh la la) .... Oh my

Oui .... (wee) .... Yes

Voilà .... (vwah-la) .... Here it is

Places

Eiffel Tower (EYE-full Tower) - A famous Paris landmark built for the 1889 World's Fair.

Notre Dame (noh-truh DAHM) - This Gothic cathedral is one of the largest and most well-known churches in the world.

Louvre Museum (LOO-vruh Museum) - One of the largest art museums, and once a royal palace.

Champs-Élysées (shawn zay-lee-ZAY) – A place of civic celebration for Parisians, and the most famous shopping street in the world.

Tuileries Garden (TWEE-luh-ree Garden) – This gorgeous public park was once the gardens of the Tuileries Palace.

Montmartre (mawn-MAR-truh) – The highest point in Paris, made famous by the artists who have lived and worked here. Home to the Sacré-Coeur Basilica.

Seine River (seyn River) – A long river winding through Paris, dividing the city into sections, the Right Bank and Left Bank.